CONTENTS
Level 10

UNIT 2: NATURALLY!

UNIT 3: THAT'S WHAT FRIENDS ARE FOR

UNIT 4: PITCH IN!

UNIT 5: MEMORIES TO KEEP

Pat Cummings: My Story

The Lucky Stone

Creation Of a California Tribe

No Star Nights

UNIT 6: TWICE-TOLD TALES

COMPOUND SUBJECTS AND COMPOUND PREDICATES

A **compound subject** is two or more simple subjects that have the same predicate. The simple subjects are joined by *and*.

Laura and Amy are experienced campers.

A **compound predicate** is two or more simple predicates that have the same subject. The simple predicates are joined by *and*.

Amy *canoes and fishes*.

Read each sentence. Underline each compound subject. Circle each compound predicate.

1. Amber, her brother Adam, and her mother were planning their camping trip.

2. They had bought and packed all their food.

3. The night before, they were sitting and talking about their trip.

4. "We have checked and double-checked everything," said Amber's mom.

5. Adam and Amber agreed with their mother.

Complete each sentence by writing a compound subject or compound predicate.

6. Grizzly bears _____.

7. _____ howled in the distance.

8. _____ shined down on the campsite.

9. Gentle waves _____.

10. _____ settled into our sleeping bags.

10   Level 10/Unit 1

Extension: Have students write three sentences with both a compound subject and a compound predicate.

15

Macmillan/McGraw-Hill

SENTENCE COMBINING

Write a paragraph about a time when a new friend came into your life. It could be an adult, a new relative, or just a friend. It could even be a pet. Use at least five compound sentences in your paragraph.

_____

_____

_____

_____

_____

_____

_____

_____

_____

_____

_____

_____

_____

_____

_____

_____

_____

_____

_____

_____

Extension: Have students reread their paragraphs and find two more sentences that can be combined.

5

COMBINING SENTENCES WITH TWO PREDICATES

> If two sentences have the same subject, they can be combined by joining the predicates.
>
> Tom *hitched up* the horses. Then Tom *plowed* the field. Tom hitched up the horses and then plowed the field.

Read each pair of sentences. Then join them by writing one sentence with a compound predicate.

1. Settlers on the prairie worked hard. The settlers went to sleep tired.

   _____

2. Prairie soil was very firm. It needed a special plow.

   _____

3. Farmers raised chickens. They grew crops, too.

   _____

4. For pets, settlers kept dogs. They also raised cats.

   _____

5. Cats were good companions. They also caught mice.

   _____

6. Prairie settlers hunted. They fished, too.

   _____

7. Horses pulled the settlers' wagons. They also dragged the plows.

   _____

8. Settlers bought supplies in town. They also met friends in town.

   _____

Extension: Have students read a paragraph in their language arts book and write down all the sentences with compound predicates.

Macmillan/McGraw-Hill

COMBINING SENTENCES WITH TWO SUBJECTS

> If two sentences have the same predicate, they can be combined by joining the subjects.
>
> The *cat* slept by the wood stove. The *dog* slept by the wood stove. The cat and dog slept by the wood stove.

Read each pair of sentences. Then join them by writing one sentence with a compound subject.

1. The horse ran over to the barrel. The colt ran over to the barrel, too.

   _____

2. The boy led the horse to the stable. The girl led the horse, too.

   _____

3. The barn is made of wood. So is the chicken coop.

   _____

4. The horses need water every day. The other animals also need water every day.

   _____

5. The horses eat hay in the winter. The sheep eat hay in the winter, too.

   _____

6. Foxes would like to get into the chicken coop. Coyotes would also like to get into the chicken coop.

   _____

7. Cleaning out the stables is a big job. So is stacking the hay in the loft.

   _____

8. Hay is cut in the summer. Straw is cut in the summer, too.

   _____

18

Extension: Have students work in pairs, with one student writing two sentences and the other combining them by using two subjects.

Level 10/Unit 1   8

Macmillan/McGraw-Hill

SENTENCE COMBINING: *AND/BUT*

> Two related sentences can be joined with a comma and *and* or *but*.
>
> The Appalachian Mountains are in the east, *and* the Rocky Mountains are in the west.

Read each pair of sentences. Then combine each pair into one sentence using the word *and* or *but*.

1. Nebraska is a prairie state. Maine is near the ocean.

   _____

2. Maine is a part of the United States. Quebec is a part of Canada.

   _____

3. Many people in Maine are sailors. Many people in Nebraska are farmers.

   _____

4. Maine has many pine trees. Nebraska has few pine trees.

   _____

5. The largest city in Maine is Portland. The largest city in Nebraska is Omaha.

   _____

6. Lincoln is the capital of Nebraska. Augusta is the capital of Maine.

   _____

7. Maine's nickname is the Pine Tree State. Nebraska's nickname is the Cornhusker State.

   _____

8. Nebraska is a large state. Maine is a small state.

   _____

Macmillan/McGraw-Hill

RUN-ONS

> A **run-on sentence** contains two or more sentences that run together.
>
> I went to the beach and I bought a soda and found some seashells.
>
> I went to the beach. I bought a soda and found some seashells.

Read each sentence. Correct each run-on by breaking it into shorter sentences.
Write the new sentences. Add capital letters and punctuation where needed.

1. My family lives in Nebraska, my parents are farmers in the western part of the
   state.

   _____

   _____

2. I have two brothers and a sister and we help out on the farm, I like living on a
   farm.

   _____

   _____

3. We raise hogs on our farm, we have about 500 sows and sows are female
   pigs.

   _____

   _____

4. We grow corn to feed to our hogs, we harvest it in the fall.

   _____

   _____

5. My favorite time is when the piglets are born, they are so cute and I like to pick
   them up, I like to hear them squeal.

   _____

   _____

NOUNS

What is your favorite wild animal? Maybe it's a tiger, a panda, or a koala. Or maybe you like dolphins, penguins, lemurs, or parrots. Write a paragraph telling about your favorite animal and why you like it. Use nouns in your paragraph.

_____

_____

_____

_____

_____

_____

_____

_____

_____

_____

_____

_____

_____

_____

_____

_____

_____

Macmillan/McGraw-Hill

WHAT IS A NOUN?

> A **noun** names a person, place, or thing.
>
> *Mr. Anderson*   *Spruce Park*   *tree*

Read each sentence. Then write all the nouns in each sentence on the line.

1. Seals have their babies on the ice. _____

2. Three different places in the world are important for the seals.

   _____

3. The seals begin their journeys in the autumn. _____

4. The author took photographs of the babies. _____

5. The photographer took a helicopter to Canada. _____

Write a sentence using the noun in parentheses.

6. (father) _____

   _____

7. (ice) _____

   _____

8. (camera) _____

   _____

9. (Canada) _____

   _____

10. (scientist) _____

   _____

COMMON NOUNS

A **common noun** names any person, place, or thing.
cousin   theater   movie

Fill in each blank with a common noun that makes sense in the paragraph.

The _____ was flying over the

_____ in northern Canada. Below, the

_____ saw only white, frozen

_____. Suddenly, a _____ in

the _____ cried, "I see the _____!"

There they were! The brown _____ stretched as far as

the _____ could see. Soon, the _____

landed in an open _____ of the ice field. The

_____ jumped out with _____.

They were _____ and had come to study the

_____. The _____ walked

toward the _____. One large _____

and her _____ looked at the approaching

_____. The _____ looked

nervous. She gave a loud _____ and waddled off. With a

_____, she and her _____

plopped through a _____ in the ice.

Extension: Have students look through a newspaper or magazine article and copy down five common nouns.

PROPER NOUNS

A **proper noun** names a particular person, place, or thing.

| *President Clinton* | *Washington, D.C.* | *Boston Celtics* |

Each important word in a proper noun begins with a capital letter.

Read each sentence. Underline each proper noun. Then write a common noun that includes the proper noun.

1. Jacques Cousteau is a famous explorer. _____

2. On his ship *Calypso,* he and his crew have sailed the world.

   _____

3. Many of his films have been shot in the Caribbean Sea.

   _____

4. John Denver wrote a song about the famous explorer's ship.

   _____

5. After his journeys, the explorer returns to his home in France.

   _____

Read the paragraph. Correct each error by drawing a slash through the noun and writing the word correctly above it.

The People who live in northern canada and alaska are called the inuit. An old

name for the inuit is the eskimos. Many inuits live a traditional life of hunting and

fishing. Others have moved to Cities or Towns. They no longer follow the traditional

Way of Life. Inuits are Citizens of canada or of the united states. The Governments

of canada and america help the inuit to keep their traditional way of life.

Extension: Have students work in pairs and make a list with two columns. In one column have a student write a common noun and the other student write a proper noun that is an example of it. Then reverse the procedure.

Level 10/Unit 2   28

Macmillan/McGraw-Hill

TITLES AND ABBREVIATIONS

An **abbreviation** is a short form of a word. Most abbreviations begin with a capital letter and end with a period. A title is an abbreviation used with a person's name.

Rewrite each sentence. Use abbreviations wherever possible.

1. Doctor Melissa A. Parmenter will give a lecture on the harp seal. _____

_____

2. The lecture will be held on September 21. _____

_____

3. The program will take place in the auditorium on Bryan Street.

_____

4. To get to the auditorium, turn left on Centennial Drive. _____

_____

5. Mister Harold Edgar will introduce the speaker. _____

_____

Match the abbreviation with the word it stands for.

Monday   August   Mister   Company   Governor

6. Aug. _____

7. Gov. _____

8. Mon. _____

9. Mr. _____

10. Co. _____

PLURAL NOUNS

Think of all the animals you know. Choose one and write a paragraph about the most amazing thing that animal does. It might be flying, swimming, jumping long distances, seeing in the dark, or hearing sounds that humans cannot hear. Use plural nouns in your paragraph.

_____

_____

_____

_____

_____

_____

_____

_____

_____

_____

_____

_____

_____

_____

_____

_____

_____

_____

_____

_____

Macmillan/McGraw-Hill

WHAT IS A PLURAL NOUN?

> A **plural noun** names more than one person, place, or thing.
> cousins   football stadiums   streets

Rewrite each sentence by changing the subject to a plural one. Change other parts of the sentence and add capital letters if necessary.

1. A large grizzly bear waits beside a stream.

_____

2. The bear's cub rolls on the ground.

_____

3. A bird chirps in a tree above the bear.

_____

4. A raccoon drinks from the stream.

_____

5. A fluffy white cloud is in the blue sky.

_____

6. A summer breeze rustles the leaves of the trees.

_____

7. A footstep echoes through the forest.

_____

8. A twig breaks with a sharp snap.

_____

Extension: Have students scan a paragraph in their social studies book and write down all the plural nouns.

Macmillan/McGraw-Hill

PLURAL NOUNS WITH -S AND -ES

Add -s to form the plural of most nouns.

  tree, trees   boat, boats

Add -es to form the plural of singular nouns that end in -s, -sh, -ch, or -x.

  pass, *passes*   lash, *lashes*   perch, *perches*   fox, *foxes*

Write the plural form of each noun.

1. dish _____

2. gas _____

3. night _____

4. rock _____

5. church _____

6. class _____

7. pitch _____

8. car _____

9. splash _____

10. fox _____

Use the plural form of each noun in parentheses in a sentence.

11. (lock) _____

12. (mix) _____

13. (wish) _____

14. (branch) _____

15. (bus) _____

28   **Extension:** Have students write four sentences, each using a plural form of a noun ending in -s, -sh, -ch, or -x.   Level 10/Unit 2   15

Macmillan/McGraw-Hill

PLURAL NOUNS WITH *-IES* AND *-EYS*

> To form the plural of nouns ending in a consonant and *-y*, change the *y* to *i* and add *-es*.
>   fly, *flies*
>
> To form the plural of nouns ending in a vowel and *-y*, add *-s*.
>   boy, *boys*

Write *C* on the line if the sentence uses plurals correctly. If the sentence uses plurals incorrectly, rewrite the plural form of the word correctly on the line.

1. Bears have their babys while they are hibernating. _____

2. Bears can make long journies to find their winter dens. _____

3. Bears will hibernate for more than a hundred days. _____

4. We read several storeys about bears. _____

5. Many citys have grizzly bears in their zoos. _____

Cross out the incorrect word. Write the correct word on the line.

6. The vallies in the national park are home to many bears.

   _____

7. Over the spring holidaies, my family went to the zoo and saw the bears.

   _____

8. The zoo keeper gives the bears nuts and blackberrys to eat.

   _____

9. The bear cubs' area contains many different toyes.

   _____

10. We put some pennys in a box by the bear area to help build a new exhibit.

    _____

15 Level 10/Unit 2

Extension: Have students read a paragraph in their social studies book and write down the plural of each noun that ends in *-y*.

29

PLURAL NOUNS

> A **plural noun** names more than one person, place, or thing.

Write *C* beside each sentence that uses plurals correctly. If the sentence uses plurals incorrectly, rewrite the plurals correctly on the lines.

1. Zooes are good places to see lots of interesting animals.

   _____

2. One area at our zoo shows the lairs of a family of foxes.

   _____

3. You can see both adults and babys in this interesting exhibit.

   _____

4. Baby foxes look a little like puppys.

   _____

5. Student can sometimes do volunteer work at the zoo.

   _____

6. One of my brother's greatest wishes is to be on the zoo volunteer staff.

   _____

7. In another area of the zoo, all sorts of birds flit around the branchs.

   _____

8. A little island in the middle of a pond is where the donkies are.

   _____

9. In another exhibit, you can wear special glasses to see animals that are active

   at night. _____

10. The zoo keeper do a great job!

   _____

Extension: Have students write an example of each kind of plural noun covered in this selection.

Level 10/Unit 2   10

Macmillan/McGraw-Hill

MORE PLURAL NOUNS

Many traditional stories explain why things are the way they are. Think about something in nature that interests you. Then use your imagination to write a paragraph explaining why this natural thing is the way it is. Use plural nouns in your paragraph.

_____

_____

_____

_____

_____

_____

_____

_____

_____

_____

_____

_____

_____

_____

_____

_____

_____

_____

_____

Macmillan/McGraw-Hill

Extension: Have students exchange paragraphs and underline the plural nouns.

NOUNS THAT FORM PLURAL BY CHANGING
-*F* OR -*FE* TO -*VES*

> To form the plural of some nouns ending in -*f* or -*fe*, change the *f* to *v* and add -*es* or -*s*.
> leaf, *leaves*   knife, *knives*

Write the plural form of each noun. Then use the noun in a sentence.

1. knife _____

_____

2. half _____

_____

3. life _____

_____

4. calf _____

_____

5. elf _____

_____

6. thief _____

_____

7. shelf _____

_____

8. wolf _____

_____

9. loaf _____

_____

Macmillan/McGraw-Hill

SPECIAL PLURAL NOUNS

Some nouns have special plural forms: man, *men*   child, *children*   ox, *oxen*.

Read each sentence. If the plural form is correct, write *C* on the line. If the plural form is incorrect, rewrite the sentence using the correct form.

1. Do you know if a frog has tooths? _____

   _____

2. How many foots does a frog have? _____

   _____

3. In some stories, animals are like children. _____

   _____

4. Two womans read our class a story. _____

   _____

5. Snakes must slither on their bellies because they have no feets. _____

   _____

6. One of those mans standing near the door is the author of the book. _____

   _____

7. He also wrote a book about a family of mouses. _____

   _____

8. In the story, the little mouse sings with two gooses. _____

   _____

9. In stories about pioneer days, two oxens pull the covered wagons. _____

   _____

10. Sometimes mules were used instead. _____

    _____

Macmillan/McGraw-Hill

SPECIAL SINGULAR AND PLURAL NOUNS

A few nouns have the same singular and plural forms.
  That *deer* ate our apples.   Several *deer* crossed the road.

Read each sentence. If the plural form is correct, write *C* on the line. If the plural form is incorrect, rewrite the sentence using the correct form.

1. The fisherman caught several salmons in the stream. _____

_____

2. Martha's family raises sheeps for the county fair. _____

_____

3. My uncle and I caught eight fish in two hours. _____

_____

4. The mooses were bellowing as loudly as they could. _____

_____

5. Reindeer live in the north of Sweden. _____

_____

6. The aquarium in the sixth-grade room has many different goldfish. _____

_____

7. Moose were the largest animals we saw in the national park. _____

_____

8. The salmon are leaping clear out of the water! _____

_____

9. Two deers suddenly jumped out into the path of the speeding car. _____

_____

10. The farmer said that sheep were his favorite farm animals. _____

_____

Extension: Have students draw pictures illustrating the special plurals in
this lesson.

Macmillan/McGraw-Hill

MORE PLURAL NOUNS

> To form the plural of some nouns ending in -*f* or -*fe*, change the *f* to *v* and add -*es* or -*s*. Some nouns have special plural forms. A few nouns have the same singular and plural forms.

Write a sentence using the plural form of the word in parentheses.

1. (knife) _____

_____

2. (man) _____

_____

3. (fish) _____

_____

4. (woman) _____

_____

5. (sheep) _____

_____

6. (wolf) _____

_____

7. (child) _____

_____

8. (deer) _____

_____

9. (calf) _____

_____

10. (mouse) _____

_____

Extension: Have students work with a partner to write the singular form of a
special noun and then supply the plural form.

POSSESSIVE NOUNS

Think about a time when you saw a large group of animals. Maybe it was fish, birds, deer, bison, or insects. Write a paragraph describing this group of animals. What did they do? How did they move? What kind of noise did they make? Use possessive nouns in your paragraph.

_____

_____

_____

_____

_____

_____

_____

_____

_____

_____

_____

_____

_____

_____

_____

_____

_____

36

Extension: Have students exchange paragraphs and underline each possessive noun.

Macmillan/McGraw-Hill

WHAT IS A POSSESSIVE NOUN?

> A **possessive noun** shows who or what owns or has something. Use apostrophes to
> form possessives.
>   *Mom's* computer   the *house's* color   the *girls'* jackets

Choose the word that correctly completes each sentence and write it on the line.

1. My sister (Amanda's, Amandas) arm is quite swollen from her bee sting.

   _____

2. Did you know that a (bees, bee's) sting can be very dangerous to some

   people? _____

3. All of a (beehive's, beehives) members have their own jobs to do.

   _____

4. It is the (drones', drones) job to eat and get fat but not to work.

   _____

5. One of (springs, spring's) signs is the sound of buzzing bees.

   _____

Write the possessive form of each underlined noun.

6. the hive of the <u>bees</u>   the _____ hive

7. the helpers of the <u>queen</u>   the _____ helpers

8. the bee sting of my <u>sister</u>   my _____ bee sting

9. a branch of a <u>tree</u>   a _____ branch

10. the job of the <u>drones</u>   the _____ job

Extension: Have students write three sentences about hawks that include
possessive nouns.

FORMING SINGULAR POSSESSIVE NOUNS

> Add an apostrophe and an -s to a singular noun to make it possessive.
>   the *puppy's* bone

Write the singular possessive form of each word.

1. autumn _____   6. worker _____

2. sky _____   7. orchard _____

3. wind _____   8. limb _____

4. current _____   9. swarm _____

5. season _____   10. air _____

Complete each sentence by writing the singular possessive form of a noun that makes sense. Use a different noun in each sentence.

11. The _____ water was very warm.

12. The _____ clearness made it easy to see to

the bottom.

13. A _____ quick movement caught my eye.

14. I could see the _____ fins very clearly.

15. The _____ rays shone through the crystal-clear water.

Extension: Have students write sentences using the singular possessive forms of
five words from the first exercise above.

Level 10/Unit 2

15

Macmillan/McGraw-Hill

FORMING PLURAL POSSESSIVE NOUNS

> Add an apostrophe to a plural noun that ends in -s to make it possessive.
>   girl *girls'*
> Add an apostrophe and an -s to form the possessive of plural nouns that do not end in -s.
>   women *women's*

Rewrite the phrase using the plural possessive form of each underlined word.

1. a gaggle of <u>geese</u> _____

2. a bed of <u>clams</u> _____

3. a pod of <u>whales</u> _____

4. a paddle of <u>ducks</u> _____

5. a brood of <u>chickens</u> _____

6. a band of <u>coyotes</u> _____

7. a colony of <u>beavers</u> _____

8. a herd of <u>deer</u> _____

9. a pride of <u>lions</u> _____

10. a school of <u>fish</u> _____

Write a sentence using the plural possessive form of the word in parentheses.

11. (field) _____

12. (sheep) _____

13. (child) _____

14. (leaf) _____

15. (pond) _____

15   Level 10/Unit 2

Extension: Have students write a sentence using the *singular* possessive form of the five words from the second exercise above.

39

POSSESSIVE NOUNS

A **possessive noun** is a noun that shows who or what owns or has something.
Add an apostrophe and an -s to a singular noun to make it possessive.
Add an apostrophe to a plural noun that ends in -s to make it possessive.
Add an apostrophe and an -s to form the possessive of plural nouns that do not end in -s.

Read the paragraph. Cross out each incorrect possessive form. On the lines below, rewrite the paragraph with correct possessive forms.

The woods behind our familys house is a very interesting place. My younger brother and my favorite thing to do is to take a walk there early in the morning. As soon as we hear the alarm clocks loud buzzing, we leap out of bed. We walk quietly past our parents room so we don't wake them up. Buddy the cats' puzzled look doesn't bother us! We put on our boots and head out the back door. The suns first rays are starting to warm up the grass. The wind rustles the trees's leaves. I hold my brothers hand when we cross the stream. Sometimes we hear a deers snorting as it runs away. The birds's singing is so loud you can barely hear anything else!

_____

_____

_____

_____

_____

_____

_____

_____

_____

_____

Extension: Have students list the possessives in the paragraph, writing both the singular and the plural forms of each one.

Level 10/Unit 2

10

Macmillan/McGraw-Hill

ACTION VERBS

Think about walking through your hometown. What are some of the interesting things you would see, hear, smell, and feel during your walk? Write a paragraph describing some of the things you would experience. Use action verbs in your paragraph.

_____

_____

_____

_____

_____

_____

_____

_____

_____

_____

_____

_____

_____

_____

_____

_____

_____

_____

_____

_____

Extension: Have students reread their paragraphs and underline each action verb. **41**

WHAT IS AN ACTION VERB (1)?

> An **action verb** is a word that expresses action. It tells what the subject does or did.
>
> Jeremy *ran*.

Read each sentence. Write each action verb on the line.

1. The police officer's dog saved the boy's life. _____

2. He walked right into traffic! _____

3. The dog jumped into the river. _____

4. He rescued the boy. _____

5. The officer praised his dog. _____

6. The dog lapped up the attention. _____

7. The training school teaches both dogs and owners. _____

8. The beagle sniffed the suspicious luggage. _____

9. The guard arrested the traveler. _____

10. The dog wiggled with excitement. _____

Write five sentences about how dogs help people. Use an action verb in each sentence.

11. _____

12. _____

13. _____

14. _____

15. _____

Extension: Have students cut pictures out of magazines that illustrate three action verbs.

15

Macmillan/McGraw-Hill

WHAT IS AN ACTION VERB (2)?

> An **action verb** is a word that expresses action. It tells what the subject does or did.

Write ten sentences using any form of the following action verbs. Cross out each verb when you use it in a sentence.

jump	write	stroll	laugh	gallop	swim	eat
yank	brush	teach	cross	hear	chase	scold

1. _____

2. _____

3. _____

4. _____

5. _____

6. _____

7. _____

8. _____

9. _____

10. _____

Extension: Have students quiz each other by writing sentences with action verbs and having a partner identify them.

ACTION VERBS: FILL IN THE BLANKS

An **action verb** is a word that expresses action. It tells what the subject does or did.

Read the paragraph. Fill in each blank with an action verb that makes sense.

Dogs _____ millions of people around the world. The trainers of these dogs _____ hours making sure the dogs learn their tasks. Police dogs _____ to find people who are lost or in danger. They _____ sniffing strange smells. And they also _____ to keep their minds on their jobs. Of course, dogs _____ mistakes. Sometimes they _____ to find the danger and _____ people in need. But these amazing creatures usually _____ themselves. They _____ us from dangerous situations.

ACTION VERBS

An **action verb** is a word that expresses action. It tells what the subject does or did.

Read the paragraph. Underline the ten action verbs and then write them on the lines below.

When a dog guide and its owner are at The Seeing Eye training school, the family goes on with their lives in a normal way. They divide the household chores. The children go to school and do their homework. Everyone prepares meals. One person vacuums the house and scrubs the kitchen floor. Another person washes the dishes and carries out the trash and cuts the grass.

_____

_____

_____

_____

_____

_____

_____

_____

_____

Extension: Have students write five action verbs and have a partner write sentences using them.

PRESENT TENSE

Everyone learns things from older people. What have you learned from a parent, a grandparent, an aunt or uncle, or some other adult? Make a list of five important lessons you have learned about life, work, being a friend, or any other subject. Use present-tense verbs in your paragraph.

1. _____
_____
_____

2. _____
_____
_____
_____

3. _____
_____
_____
_____

4. _____
_____
_____
_____

5. _____
_____
_____
_____

Extension: Have students exchange lists with a partner and underline all the present-tense verbs in each other's paragraphs.

SINGULAR SUBJECTS: ADD -S OR -ES

A verb in the **present tense** tells what happens now. When you use present-tense verbs with a singular subject, add -s to most verbs.
  run, *runs*
Add -es to verbs that end in -s, -ch, -sh, -x, or -z.
  pass, *passes*   twitch, *twitches*   push, *pushes*   fix, *fixes*   buzz, *buzzes*
Change -y to i and add -es to verbs that end in a consonant and -y.
  hurry, *hurries*

Read each sentence. Circle the word in parentheses that correctly completes the sentence.

1. Aunt Millie (mix, mixes) the pancakes carefully.

2. She (checks, check) the stove.

3. Sally (fries, fry) the bacon.

4. Julia (think, thinks) it smells delicious!

5. She (watches, watchs) Aunt Millie work.

6. A mosquito (buzzs, buzzes) around Julia's head.

7. A cat (meowies, meows) and flicks its tail.

8. Aunt Millie (washs, washes) the breakfast dishes.

9. Julia (misses, miss) her brother.

10. Julia (worreys, worries) about the kittens.

Macmillan/McGraw-Hill

10   Level 10/Unit 3

Extension: Have students take turns writing sentences with present-tense verbs and identifying the verb.

47

PLURAL SUBJECTS: DO NOT ADD -S OR -ES

> Do not add -s or -es to a present-tense verb when the subject is plural or *I* or *you*.
> I *walk*.   You *walk*.

Read each sentence. Then rewrite it to make the subject plural. Change the verb and any other words if you need to.

1. The horse shakes its head in anger. _____

_____

2. The boy smooths the covers on his bed. _____

_____

3. The opossum carries its babies on its back. _____

_____

4. A fly buzzes around Grandpa's head. _____

_____

5. The cowboy fixes the fence. _____

_____

6. An animal splashes in the stream. _____

_____

7. A rattlesnake catches a mouse. _____

_____

8. The boy passes the biscuits to his grandfather. _____

_____

9. The cook stews the raisins. _____

_____

10. The ranch hand hurries to finish the job. _____

_____

48   **Extension:** Have students write five sentences using a plural present-tense verb
and then change them to singular.

Level 10/Unit 3   10

Macmillan/McGraw-Hill

SINGULAR AND PLURAL SUBJECTS

> When you use present-tense verbs with a singular subject, add -s to most verbs.
> Add -es to verbs that end in -s, -ch, -sh, -x, or -z.
> Change y to i and add -es to verbs that end in a consonant and -y.
> Do not add -s or -es to a present-tense verb when the subject is plural or I or you.

Write two different present-tense sentences using each verb shown. The first sentence should have I, you, or a plural noun as the subject. The second sentence should have he, she, it, or a singular noun as the subject. After you have written the sentences, underline the part of the verb that changed.

1. toss _____

_____

_____

2. switch _____

_____

_____

3. bury _____

_____

_____

4. eat _____

_____

_____

5. poke _____

_____

_____

Extension: Have students read a paragraph in their social studies book and write down all the present-tense verbs.

PRESENT TENSE

> When you use present-tense verbs with a singular subject, add -s to most verbs.
> Add -es to verbs that end in -s, -ch, -sh, -x, or -z.
> Change y to i and add -es to verbs that end in a consonant and -y.
> Do not add -s or -es to a present-tense verb when the subject is plural or I or you.

Read the paragraph. Underline each present-tense singular verb. Circle each present-tense plural verb. Draw an arrow to the subject of each verb.

My grandfather works on a ranch out west. My brother and I visit him each summer. We help Grandpa with some of his chores. He rides fence in the mornings. Grandpa inspects the ranch's fences. Then he marks on a map the spots to repair. Men from the ranch fix the fence later. Our grandfather makes the best lunches! His biscuits taste fantastic. He fries salt pork perfectly. I work up a big appetite out on the range. My brother gets awfully hungry, too. Even the horses need lunch and a drink of water. I take them to the stream, and they drink for a long time. Then my brother gives them some grain to eat. Finally, our turn comes, and we eat our lunch. The biscuits go fast! The salt pork disappears, too. After lunch, we all clean up. I wash the dishes, and Grandpa dries them. My brother puts them back in the shed. Then we ride off onto the range.

Extension: Have students write three sentences describing what they have done today, using *I* as the subject. Then have them rewrite the sentences, changing the subject to *he, she,* or *they.*

50

PAST TENSE

Have you ever had a misunderstanding with a friend? It can happen to anybody. Write a paragraph about such a time. What was the misunderstanding about? How did it happen? How did you solve the problem? Use past-tense verbs in your paragraph.

_____

_____

_____

_____

_____

_____

_____

_____

_____

_____

_____

_____

_____

_____

_____

_____

_____

_____

_____

_____

Macmillan/McGraw-Hill

Extension: Have students reread their paragraphs and underline each past-tense verb.

VERBS IN THE PAST: ADD -ED

Add -ed to most verbs to show **past tense**.
   jump, *jumped*
If a verb ends in -e, drop the e and add -ed.
   chase, *chased*

Complete each sentence by writing the past-tense form of a verb that makes sense. Choose from among the following verbs. Use each verb only once.

want   love   hunt   sail   land   elect   help   present   ask   plant

1. Our class _____ a play about the Pilgrims.

2. The Pilgrims _____ in Massachusetts in 1620.

3. They _____ on a ship called the *Mayflower*.

4. Indians living in Massachusetts _____ the Pilgrims during the first hard winter.

5. The Pilgrims _____ corn, potatoes, and other crops.

6. They also _____ for wild game such as deer, rabbits, and ducks.

7. The Pilgrims _____ Miles Standish to be their army commander.

8. Captain Standish _____ the beautiful Priscilla.

9. Captain Standish _____ his friend John Alden to speak to Priscilla.

10. But Priscilla _____ to marry John Alden instead!

Extension: Have students listen to a news broadcast and write down as many past-tense verbs as they can.

Level 10/Unit 3   10

Macmillan/McGraw-Hill

VERBS IN THE PAST: CHANGE -Y TO I AND ADD -ED

> If a verb ends with a consonant and -y, change the -y to i and add -ed.
>   try, *tried* carry, *carried*

Circle the word in parentheses that correctly completes the sentence.

1. Ms. Rodriguez (worryed, worried) about the snowstorm.

2. Felipe (tried, tryed) to reach the window.

3. We (carryed, carried) the bags of trash out to the curb.

4. His dog Pepe (buried, buryed) a slipper in the backyard.

5. I (hurried, hurryed) home after school.

Read each sentence. Then rewrite it in the past tense, using the correct form of the underlined verb. Change any other words as needed.

6. Aunt Jane <u>replies</u> quickly when I send her a letter. _____

   _____

7. If my sister <u>marries</u> the gym teacher, he'll be my brother-in-law! _____

   _____

8. The suspect <u>denies</u> that she committed the crime. _____

   _____

9. Her brother <u>studies</u> very hard. _____

   _____

10. A horse <u>whinnies</u> when I go into the stable. _____

   _____

Macmillan/McGraw-Hill

⟋10⟋ Level 10/Unit 3

Extension: Have students quiz each other by writing a sentence in present tense and having a partner rewrite it into the past tense.

53

VERBS IN THE PAST: DOUBLE THE FINAL CONSONANT AND ADD -ED

> If a verb ends with one vowel and one consonant, double the consonant and add -ed.
>   prop, *propped*

Write a paragraph about a project your class has done at school. Use at least five of the verbs in the box in the past tense.

stub	rap	plan	hug	drag	stop
rub	flop	jam	hum	plop	pet	clap

_____

_____

_____

_____

_____

_____

_____

_____

_____

_____

_____

_____

_____

Extension: Have students exchange paragraphs and underline the past-tense verbs.

Macmillan/McGraw-Hill

PAST TENSE

A verb in the past tense tells what happened earlier.
Add -ed to most verbs to show past tense.
If a verb ends with a consonant and -y, change the -y to i and add -ed.
If a verb ends with one vowel and one consonant, double the consonant and add -ed.

Use the following diagram to make a chart of how different verbs form their past tenses. Read the rule in each box. Then list five verbs you know that form their past tenses according to the rule.

1. Add -ed to most verbs.	2. If a verb ends with -e, drop the e and add -ed.	3. If a verb ends with a consonant and -y, change the y to i and add -ed.	4. If a verb ends with one vowel and one consonant, double the consonant and add -ed.
1.	1.	1.	1.
2.	2.	2.	2.
3.	3.	3.	3.
4.	4.	4.	4.
5.	5.	5.	5.

Macmillan/McGraw-Hill

Extension: Have students write sentences using the past tense of a verb in each category.

HAVE, BE, DO

Everybody is different, but people still become close friends. Think of a friend of yours who is different from you. Maybe this friend looks different, acts different, or enjoys some different things. Write a paragraph explaining how you can still be friends in spite of your differences. Use the verbs *be, have,* and *do* in your paragraph.

_____

_____

_____

_____

_____

_____

_____

_____

_____

_____

_____

_____

_____

_____

_____

_____

_____

_____

_____

_____

_____

_____

Extension: Have students reread their paragraphs and underline each use of *be, have,* and *do.*

USING *HAVE*

> Use *has* and *had* to tell about one person or thing.
> Jack *has* a new football. He *had* it at the game.
> Use *have* and *had* to tell about more than one person or thing.
> Fred and Jamal *have* new shoes. They *had* to get a bigger size.

Read each sentence. Circle the word in parentheses that correctly completes the sentence.

1. My grandfather (has, have) a baseball autographed by Jackie Robinson.

2. He and Grandma (have, has) the ball on their bookshelf.

3. Jackie Robinson (has, had) a hard time when he first joined the Dodgers.

4. He (have, had) to listen to nasty language.

5. Justin's dad (have, has) a baseball card of Jackie Robinson.

6. My cousins (has, have) a card of Pee Wee Reese.

7. Justin's father (had, have) a lot of trouble finding his baseball card.

8. You (has, have) a baseball card of Ken Griffey, Jr., don't you?

9. Ken Griffey (has, had) a fantastic season last year!

10. My sister (have, has) a signed photograph of Ken Griffey, Jr., her favorite

    baseball player.

10 Level 10/Unit 3

Extension: Have students write a sentence about baseball using each of the three forms of the verb *have*.

57

USING *BE*

> Use *is* and *was* to tell about one person or thing.
>   Baseball *is* the All-American sport. The game *was* in Cleveland.
> Use *are* and *were* to tell about more than one person or thing.
>   We *are* all going to the game. They *were* there with the tickets.

Complete each sentence by writing in the correct form of the verb *be.*

1. Cal Ripken, Jr., of the Baltimore Orioles _____ my

   favorite baseball player.

2. Brooks Robinson _____ a star for the Orioles in

   the 1960s.

3. Josh Gibson and Satchel Paige _____ two stars of

   the old Negro League.

4. Both Gibson and Paige _____ now in the Baseball

   Hall of Fame.

5. Baseball _____ only for white players for many years.

6. Cleveland's Albert Belle, one of today's greatest stars,

   _____ an African American.

7. Many of baseball's best players today _____ from

   Mexico, Puerto Rico, and other Latin American countries.

8. Roberto Clemente _____ a great Puerto Rican star

   for the Pittsburgh Pirates in the 1960s and 1970s.

9. Last year, my brother and I _____ big ice hockey fans.

10. Now, my brother and I _____ very interested in

    baseball.

Extension: Have students listen to a favorite song and write down forms of the
verb *be* that occur in it.   Level 10/Unit 3   10

Macmillan/McGraw-Hill

USING Do

> Use *does* and *did* to tell about one person or thing.
>   Joan *does* well at soccer. I *did* all the problems.
> Use *do* and *did* to tell about more than one person or thing.
>   We *do* many fun crafts at camp. They *did* their best.

Complete each sentence by writing in *does, do,* or *did.*

1. People _____ many brave things.

2. No African American played in the major leagues until Jackie Robinson

   _____.

3. People _____ many cruel things to the Dodger star.

4. Some people still _____ cruel things today.

5. _____ your grandfather remember seeing Jackie
   Robinson in the World Series?

Write five sentences about a person you respect and admire. Use a form of *do* in
each sentence.

6. _____

_____

7. _____

_____

8. _____

_____

9. _____

_____

10. _____

_____

Extension: Have students read a page of a favorite book and write down each use
of the verb *do.*

Macmillan/McGraw-Hill

HAVE, BE, DO

Use *has, had, is, was, does,* and *did* to tell about one person or thing.
Use *have, had, are, were, do,* and *did* to tell about more than one person or thing.

Write ten sentences about your favorite sport or activity. Use the form of *have, be,* or *do* given in parentheses.

1. (have) _____

_____

2. (did) _____

_____

3. (are) _____

_____

4. (has) _____

_____

5. (does) _____

_____

6. (was) _____

_____

7. (do) _____

_____

8. (were) _____

_____

9. (had) _____

_____

10. (is) _____

60

Extension: Have students read a newspaper article from the sports section and circle each use of *be, have,* and *do.*

Level 10/Unit 3

10

Macmillan/McGraw-Hill

MAIN AND HELPING VERBS

People can make their neighborhoods better places to live. Think of a project that would be a good one for your neighborhood or town. Maybe you need a community center, playground, or ball field. Maybe you need to raise money for a cause. Write a paragraph about the project. Explain why you think it is a good one for your community. Use main and helping verbs in your paragraph.

_____

_____

_____

_____

_____

_____

_____

_____

_____

_____

_____

_____

_____

_____

_____

_____

_____

_____

Macmillan/McGraw-Hill

Extension: Have students reread their paragraphs and underline each main verb and circle each helping verb.

WHAT IS A MAIN VERB?

A **main verb** shows what the subject is or does.
  I have *walked* to school every day this week.
  They were *riding* their bikes.

Read each sentence. Write the main verb on the line.

1. Our neighborhood is planning a community garden. _____

2. I am helping with the digging and cleanup. _____

3. The city has torn down an old building. _____

4. This building had sat empty for several years. _____

5. Trucks have carried away the last of the trash from the vacant lot. _____

6. Everyone in the neighborhood was watching the cleanup. _____

7. We have worked hard getting our garden ready. _____

8. Even the dogs and cats have helped! _____

9. We will plant tomatoes, carrots, beans, and pumpkins. _____

10. I am hoping for a good crop in our first year! _____

Extension: Ask students to read several paragraphs in a favorite book and write down ten main verbs they find.

Macmillan/McGraw-Hill

WHAT IS A HELPING VERB?

A **helping verb** helps the main verb show an action or make a statement. Common helping verbs are *am, is, are, was, were, have, has, had,* and *will.*
   I *am* going today.   They *will* meet us tomorrow.

Read each sentence. Write the helping verb on the line. Underline the main verb.

1. My family has lived in this neighborhood for more than 20 years. _____

2. We have joined the neighborhood association. _____

3. My sister and I are helping on the playground this summer. _____

4. I am supervising the art class for kindergarteners. _____

5. My sister is helping with the softball team. _____

6. The team will play in a tournament later this month. _____

7. The players are practicing three times a week. _____

8. My art class was working with clay, paints, and printmaking. _____

9. They had decided to enter the city art fair. _____

10. We will help at the playground until August. _____

Extension: Have students listen to the words of a favorite song and write down five helping verbs they hear in the lyrics.

PRACTICE WITH MAIN AND HELPING VERBS

A **main verb** shows what the subject is or does.
A **helping verb** helps the main verb show an action or make a statement.
Common helping verbs are *am, is, are, was, were, have, has, had,* and *will.*

Read each sentence. If a main verb is missing, write *M* on the first line. If a helping verb is missing, write *H*. Then write the missing part on the line.

_____ 1. Mr. Menendez _____ weeding his garden last night.

_____ 2. He and his family have _____ a garden for many years.

_____ 3. This year they are _____ corn, potatoes, and peppers.

_____ 4. In the past, they _____ planted broccoli, squash, and celery, too.

_____ 5. Several neighborhood kids _____ helping Mr. Menendez work in his garden last week.

_____ 6. "What's the biggest pumpkin you have ever

_____?" one boy asked Mr. Menendez.

_____ 7. "I was _____ to lift it and I needed a dump truck!" he answered with a laugh.

_____ 8. We _____ all laughing so hard we couldn't stop!

_____ 9. "_____ you plant another garden next year?" one girl asked.

_____ 10. "We are _____ to have a garden next year and every year," Mr. Menendez answered.

Extension: Have students write the helping verbs they added in one column and the main verbs in a second. Then have them combine the verbs into five new sentences.

64

Level 10/Unit 4

20

Macmillan/McGraw-Hill

MAIN AND HELPING VERBS

> A **main verb** shows what the subject is or does.
> A **helping verb** helps the main verb to show an action or make a statement.
> Common helping verbs are *am, is, are, was, were, have, has, had,* and *will.*

Using the main verb or helping verb in parentheses, write a sentence with both a main and a helping verb.

1. (explore) _____

_____

2. (will) _____

_____

3. (send) _____

_____

4. (answer) _____

_____

5. (had) _____

_____

6. (are) _____

_____

7. (shout) _____

_____

8. (is) _____

_____

9. (dream) _____

10. (have) _____

_____

Extension: Have students make a chart of the common helping verbs and write a sentence using each one.

LINKING VERBS

Have you ever wanted to go on a whale-watching trip? Write a description of what you might see. Describe the boat, the sea, the captain or guide, the passengers, and, of course, the whales. Use linking verbs in your paragraph.

_____

_____

_____

_____

_____

_____

_____

_____

_____

_____

_____

_____

_____

_____

_____

_____

_____

_____

BE IN THE PRESENT

> A **linking verb** does not show action. It connects the subject to the rest of the sentence.
> *Is, am,* and *are* are present-tense linking verbs.
>   Leo *is* happy.   I *am* pleased.   They *are* my friends.

Read each sentence. Circle the word in parentheses that correctly completes the sentence.

1. (Whales, Whale) are the largest animals that have ever lived on Earth.

2. The blue whale (is, are) the largest of the whales.

3. That woman (am, is) a guide on a whale-watching boat.

4. The (oceans, ocean) off the coast of Massachusetts is a good place to see whales.

5. The narwhal's horn (are, is) a fascinating subject.

6. Another name for this whale (am, is) the unicorn whale.

7. A popular attraction at the sea park (is, are) the killer whale.

8. These animals (is, are) beautiful black-and-white creatures.

9. The (visitor, visitors) are interested in the whales.

10. I (am, are) excited about seeing a live whale.

Extension: Have students write out the lyrics to a favorite song and underline each linking verb.

BE IN THE PAST

> A **linking verb** does not show action. It connects the subject to the rest of the sentence.
> *Was* and *were* are past-tense linking verbs.
>   Tina *was* late.   Kim and Lena *were* ready.

Read each sentence. Write in the past-tense linking verb that correctly completes the sentence.

1. The boat _____ ready to leave the dock.

2. Waves _____ already very rough.

3. The guide _____ a professor from the university.

4. I _____ hopeful we would see a whale.

5. All the passengers _____ thrilled!

Write a sentence using the subject and the past-tense linking verb *was* or *were*.

6. Shannon and Maria _____

_____

7. A narwhal _____

_____

8. You _____

_____

9. The whale-watching trip _____

_____

10. Several humpback whales _____

_____

Extension: Have students look through a short section of their social studies book and copy all the past-tense linking verbs.

Level 10/Unit 4

10

Macmillan/McGraw-Hill

BE IN THE FUTURE

A **linking verb** does not show action. It connects the subject to the rest of the sentence. *Will be* is a future-tense linking verb.
   John *will be* twelve next week.

Rewrite each sentence using the future-tense linking verb *will be*. Change any other words as needed.

1. The ocean is very calm tonight. _____

2. I am on the main deck of the boat. _____

3. My sister and I were the first to sign up for this trip. _____

    _____

4. We are members of the Nature Club at school. _____

    _____

5. The leader of the trip was Ms. Jackson. _____

    _____

6. Many Nature Club members are interested in whale-watching. _____

    _____

7. I am vice president of the club this year. _____

    _____

8. My sister was club president last year. _____

    _____

9. My favorite whale is the gray whale. _____

    _____

10. Ms. Jackson and I were hopeful that we would see one on this trip. _____

    _____

Extension: Have students work in pairs to write sentences. Have one student write a linking-verb sentence in one of the three tenses and the other change the sentence's tense.

LINKING VERBS

A **linking verb** does not show action. It connects the subject to the rest of the sentence.
Is, am, are, was, were, and *will be* are linking verbs.

Complete each sentence by writing the correct linking verb in the blank. Then underline the subject of the sentence.

1. Kristen _____ late for the Nature Club meeting tomorrow.

2. Many members _____ unhappy when last month's meeting was cancelled.

3. I _____ sure you will enjoy this movie about whales.

4. The film _____ in color and takes 25 minutes.

5. William and Martin _____ today's speakers.

6. Sarah _____ in charge of last January's meeting.

7. Whales _____ one of my favorite animals.

8. Whales _____ my favorite animals for many years to come.

9. Tonight's meeting _____ just about to start.

10. Sarah and I _____ happy when we learned the film was about whales.

Macmillan/McGraw-Hill

IRREGULAR VERBS

What might happen if people do not take care of the environment? Think about a time when you helped protect the environment. Maybe you recycled paper or glass, picked up trash and litter, or worked with animals. Write a paragraph describing what you did, who helped you, and how it made you feel. Use irregular verbs in your paragraph.

_____

_____

_____

_____

_____

_____

_____

_____

_____

_____

_____

_____

_____

_____

_____

_____

Extension: Have students exchange paragraphs and underline each
irregular verb.

IRREGULAR VERBS USING *HAVE*, *HAS*, OR *HAD*: PAST TENSE

Some verbs have special spellings when used with *have, has,* or *had*. The following chart shows some of these verbs.

Present Tense	Form with *Have*, *Has*, or *Had*
go	gone
come	come
begin	begun
run	run
do	done
eat	eaten
give	given
grow	grown
see	seen
sing	sung

Read each sentence. Circle the word in parentheses that correctly completes the sentence.

1. I have (went, gone) with my mother to the recycling station.

2. Our family has (begun, begin) to recycle paper, glass, and plastic.

3. The tree our class planted has (growed, grown) a foot since last year.

4. I have (seen, saw) litter and trash behind the school building.

5. What has our class (did, done) about this trash?

Extension: Have students use the following verbs in a past-tense sentence with *have, has,* or *had: come, run, eat, sing,* and *give.*

5

Macmillan/McGraw-Hill

IRREGULAR VERBS (1): PAST TENSE

> Some verbs have special spellings to show past tense. Some of these verbs and their past-tense forms are *go (went), come (came), begin (began), run (ran),* and *do (did).*

Rewrite each sentence in the past tense. Change the verb and any other words as needed.

1. Earth Week begins today at our school. _____

_____

2. We do many different activities to celebrate Earth Week. _____

_____

3. Nina and Leo go to a city council meeting to talk about recycling. _____

_____

4. Some people in the class run in a special Earth Week race. _____

_____

5. A professor from the college will come to speak about water pollution today.

_____

Write a sentence using the past tense of the verb in parentheses.

6. (do) _____

7. (begin) _____

8. (go) _____

9. (run) _____

10. (come) _____

IRREGULAR VERBS (2): PAST TENSE

Some verbs have special spellings to show past tense. Some of these verbs and their past-tense forms are *eat (ate), give (gave), grow (grew), see (saw),* and *sing (sang).*

Rewrite each sentence in the past tense. Change the verb and any other words as needed.

1. That scientist gives a talk to our class about electric cars.

   _____

2. The governor sees how important protecting the environment is.

   _____

3. Weeds grow in the vacant lot next to the school. _____

   _____

4. We often eat our lunch outside on nice days. _____

   _____

5. The choir sings "America the Beautiful." _____

   _____

Write a sentence using the past tense of the verb in parentheses.

6. (see) _____

7. (grow) _____

8. (give) _____

9. (sing) _____

10. (eat) _____

Extension: Have students change each sentence they wrote in the second exercise to the past tense with *have, has,* or *had.*

10

IRREGULAR VERBS

Some verbs have special spellings when used in the past tense and when used with *have, has,* or *had.*

Fill in the missing forms for present tense, past tense, and past tense with *have, has,* or *had.*

Present Tense	**Past Tense**	**Form with** Have, Has, **or** Had
go	1. _____	2. _____
3. _____	came	4. _____
5. _____	6. _____	begun
7. _____	ran	8. _____
do	9. _____	10. _____
eat	11. _____	12. _____
13. _____	14. _____	given
15. _____	grew	16. _____
17. _____	18. _____	seen
sing	19. _____	20. _____

Extension: Have students make flash cards with these ten irregular verbs to practice the past-tense forms.

CONTRACTIONS

Environmentalists find ways to help our world. Some help change laws, others entertain us with music, books, or movies, and still others find cures for diseases or invent helpful products. Write a paragraph describing one person you admire who has helped the world in some way. Use contractions in your paragraph.

_____

_____

_____

_____

_____

_____

_____

_____

_____

_____

_____

_____

_____

_____

_____

_____

_____

_____

_____

_____

_____

WHAT IS A CONTRACTION?

A **contraction** is a shortened form of two words. An **apostrophe** (') shows where one or more letters have been left out of a contraction.
Some contractions are *I'm, you're, she's, it's, we're, isn't, can't, don't, won't, hasn't, haven't, wouldn't,* and *couldn't.*

Read each sentence. Underline each contraction. Then write on the line the words that the contraction combines.

1. The workers couldn't clean up all the spilled oil.

   _____

2. It's important to work carefully. _____

3. Protecting the environment isn't always easy. _____

4. Some people won't help on the litter project. _____

5. Most people don't want the air polluted. _____

6. I know you're interested in recycling. _____

7. She can't make it to the meeting on Friday. _____

8. I'm going to take notes for her. _____

9. The meeting hasn't started yet. _____

10. We're picking up trash along the river this week.

    _____

Extension: Have students write three sentences about what their family does to help the environment. Make sure they use a different contraction in each sentence.

CONTRACTIONS WITH A SUBJECT PRONOUN AND VERB

A **contraction** is a shortened form of two words. An **apostrophe** (') shows where one or more letters have been left out of a contraction. Some contractions are *I'm, she's, he's, it's, we're, you're, they're, I've, you've, we've,* and *they've.*

Read each sentence. Then rewrite it using a contraction for the underlined words.

1. <u>We are</u> very interested in ponds and lakes. _____

   _____

2. <u>She is</u> a volunteer at the state park. _____

   _____

3. <u>I am</u> going on a hike this Saturday. _____

   _____

4. <u>It is</u> snowing today. _____

   _____

5. <u>They have</u> collected leaves for a class project. _____

   _____

6. <u>You are</u> coming to the Nature club meeting. _____

   _____

7. <u>He is</u> taking the newspapers to the recycling center. _____

   _____

8. <u>They are</u> in a big pile in the garage. _____

   _____

9. <u>You have</u> read parts of *Silent Spring* by Rachel Carson. _____

   _____

10. <u>It is</u> important to pick up all the trash. _____

    _____

Macmillan/McGraw-Hill

CONTRACTIONS WITH *NOT*

A **contraction** is a shortened form of two words. An **apostrophe** (') shows where one or more letters have been left out of a contraction. Some contractions with *not* are *isn't, can't, don't, doesn't, won't, hasn't, haven't, wouldn't, shouldn't,* and *couldn't.*

Read each sentence. Then rewrite it using one of the contractions listed in the box above.

1. Recycling glass and plastic does not take a lot of time. _____

_____

2. Felipe could not help clean up the park last week. _____

_____

3. Some people do not recycle their old newspapers. _____

_____

4. I would not touch that liquid if I were you. _____

_____

5. Factories cannot dump wastes into the lake. _____

_____

6. Fish will not live in polluted water. _____

7. The air here has not become polluted. _____

_____

8. Drivers should not throw papers out of their cars. _____

_____

9. It is not smart to litter the playground. _____

_____

10. My brother and I have not attended a meeting yet. _____

_____

Extension: Have students make flash cards to practice the contractions in this section.

CONTRACTIONS

A **contraction** is a shortened form of two words. An **apostrophe** (') shows where one or more letters have been left out of a contraction. Some contractions are *I'm, he's, she's, it's, we're, you're, they're, isn't, can't, don't, doesn't, won't, hasn't, haven't, wouldn't, shouldn't,* and *couldn't.*

Solve the crossword puzzle using the clues. Write in the blanks the words that the contraction in the clue stands for. Don't leave spaces between the words.

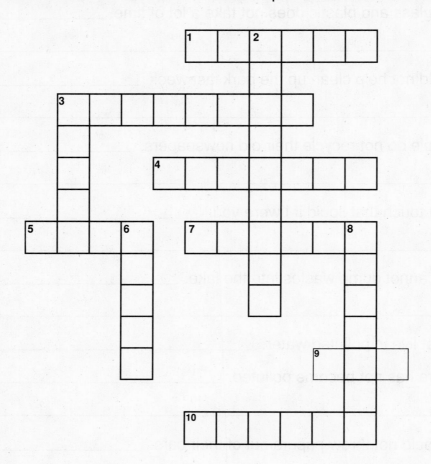

Across

1. hasn't

3. wouldn't

4. won't

5. he's

7. can't

9. I'm

10. you're

Down

2. shouldn't

3. we're

6. she's

8. they're

Extension: Have students write a sentence using five of the contractions in the puzzle.

Level 10/Unit 4   10

Macmillan/McGraw-Hill

PRONOUNS

Illustrators get ideas about what to draw from the people, places, and things they see. How do you get ideas for what you draw? Write a paragraph describing people, places, and things you like to draw. Tell why they interest you and what sorts of things you like to draw best. Use pronouns in your paragraph.

_____

_____

_____

_____

_____

_____

_____

_____

_____

_____

_____

_____

_____

_____

_____

_____

_____

WHAT ARE SUBJECT AND OBJECT PRONOUNS?

Use a **subject pronoun** (*I, you, he, she, it, we, they*) as the subject of a sentence.
   I love to draw.
Use an **object pronoun** (*me, you, him, her, it, us, them*) after an action verb or after words such as *for, at, of, with,* and *to.*
   It was time for *me* to go home.

Read the paragraph. Circle the word in parentheses that correctly completes the sentence.

   Last night (I, me) looked through an old family scrapbook. In (them, it) were some old drawings that my great-grandfather had made a long time ago. (He, Him) lived in Mexico and liked to draw people and places in his town. His sister is in many of the drawings. (She, Her) is a small girl with dark hair and eyes. (Her, She) is usually smiling. (Me, I) have a favorite drawing in the scrapbook. Great-grandfather's sister is standing near a burro. (She, He) is giving an apple to (he, him). (It, They) is bright red with green leaves still attached. The burro is wearing a big yellow hat called a sombrero. Here is the reason I like this drawing the best: the girl in the picture looks just like (me, I)!

Extension: Over each pronoun they circled, have students write whether it is a subject pronoun(*S*) or an object pronoun(*O*).

Macmillan/McGraw-Hill

SINGULAR AND PLURAL SUBJECT PRONOUNS

Add -s to most action verbs in the present when you use the pronouns *he, she,* and *it.*
   She draws.
Do not add -s to most action verbs in the present when you use the pronouns *I, we, you,* and *they.*
   I draw.

Complete each sentence using the correct present-tense form of the action verb in parentheses.

1. (ride) They _____

2. (eat) She _____

3. (take) I _____

4. (turn) It _____

5. (choose) He _____

6. (draw) You _____

7. (imagine) We _____

8. (say) It _____

9. (watch) They _____

10. (drink) She _____

Extension: Have students look through a magazine article and write out each subject pronoun.

SINGULAR AND PLURAL OBJECT PRONOUNS

Use an object pronoun *(me, you, him, her, it, us, them)* after an action verb and after words such as *for, at, of, with,* and *to.*
   She *drew them* in red hats.
   The picture was *for them*.

Read each sentence. Circle the word in parentheses that correctly completes the sentence.

   1. (Us, We) read this book in class.

   2. I admire the artist and sent a letter to (him, he).

   3. He sent a picture and a letter back to (me, I).

   4. Did you tell (she, her) the secret?

   5. I can't go to the art club meeting with (you, your).

   6. Drawing is hard, but you'll get the hang of (it, its) soon.

   7. Could you give your autograph to (we, us)?

   8. Please put (them, they) on the art supplies shelf.

   9. Monique saw (she, her) at the student art gallery.

   10. (Them, They) will meet Martin at the art room.

Extension: Have students listen to the words of a favorite song and write each object pronoun they hear.

Level 10/Unit 5   10

Macmillan/McGraw-Hill

USING *I* AND *ME*

I is a subject pronoun. *Me* is an object pronoun. When you use *I* and one or more other subject pronouns, *I* should come last. Always capitalize *I*.
    Sara and I worked together.
When you use *me* and one or more other object pronouns, *me* should come last.
    The award went to *her and me.*

Read each pair of sentences. Place a check mark before the one in each pair that correctly uses *I* or *me*.

1a. _____ She chose me to work on the posters for the art club.

b. _____ She chose I to work on the posters for the art club.

2a. _____ Lawrence, Shayla, and me are entering the art contest.

b. _____ Lawrence, Shayla, and I are entering the art contest.

3a. _____ Are you going to come with me and Tim?

b. _____ Are you going to come with Tim and me?

4a. _____ I and Ramon are the best drawers in the class.

b. _____ Ramon and I are the best drawers in the class.

5a. _____ That artist sent a drawing to my mom and me.

b. _____ That artist sent a drawing to my mom and I.

6a. _____ My dad is taking I to the exhibit of children's book art.

b. _____ My dad is taking me to the exhibit of children's book art.

7a. _____ My grandmother and me like the same kind of paintings.

b. _____ My grandmother and I like the same kind of paintings.

8a. _____ I think that postcard is for me.

b. _____ I think that postcard is for I.

9a. _____ Do you think i can still enter the art contest?

b. _____ Do you think I can still enter the art contest?

10a. _____ That painting doesn't make any sense at all to I.

b. _____ That painting doesn't make any sense at all to me.

Macmillan/McGraw-Hill

10   Level 10/Unit 5

Extension: Have students write a paragraph about gifts they have given and received. Then have students exchange paragraphs and mark each subject and object pronoun.

85

POSSESSIVE PRONOUNS

Do you have a favorite possession? Maybe it's a good-luck charm, a piece of clothing, or just something interesting you found and kept. Write a paragraph about this favorite thing. Tell how you got it, why you like it, and anything else about it you want to include. Use possessive pronouns in your paragraph.

_____

_____

_____

_____

_____

_____

_____

_____

_____

_____

_____

_____

_____

_____

_____

_____

_____

_____

86 **Extension:** Have students reread their paragraphs and underline each possessive pronoun.

WHAT ARE POSSESSIVE PRONOUNS?

A **possessive pronoun** takes the place of a possessive noun.
Possessive pronouns are *my, your, yours, his, her, hers, its, our, ours, their, theirs,* and *mine.*
  Bill's kite.   *His* kite.

Read each sentence. Then rewrite it, replacing the underlined words with a possessive pronoun and any other necessary words.

1. Have any of you seen <u>Melanie's</u> lucky rock? _____

   _____

2. That dancing dog <u>belongs to me</u>. _____

   _____

3. <u>Jim Hays's</u> drawings add a lot to the book. _____

   _____

4. <u>The girls'</u> dresses are wonderful. _____

   _____

5. They were frightened of <u>the dog's</u> snarl. _____

   _____

6. Those books <u>belong to them</u>. _____

   _____

7. Please don't touch <u>Michael's and my</u> display. _____

   _____

8. The book report <u>belongs to Natalie and me</u>. _____

   _____

9. "This is <u>Richard's</u> big chance," Richard said to himself. _____

   _____

10. The books on the desk are <u>Stephanie's</u>. _____

   _____

---

10 Level 10/Unit 5

Extension: Have students mark above each pronoun they wrote whether it comes before a noun (*B*) or stands alone (*A*).

POSSESSIVE PRONOUNS USED BEFORE NOUNS

Sometimes possessive pronouns are used before nouns: *my, your, his, her, its, our, their.*

   Her hat is red.

Write in a possessive pronoun that correctly completes each sentence.

1. Were you proud when _____ drawing won the contest?

2. I visited _____ great-grandmother over the weekend.

3. The dog licked _____ hurt paw.

4. The dancing dogs finished _____ act and left the stage.

5. Mr. Chan made _____ announcements over the loudspeaker.

Write a sentence using the possessive pronoun in parentheses.

6. (her) _____

_____

7. (their) _____

_____

8. (its) _____

_____

9. (our) _____

_____

10. (your) _____

_____

Extension: Have students listen to the words of a favorite song and write down the possessive pronouns that precede a noun.

Level 10/Unit 5

10

Macmillan/McGraw-Hill

POSSESSIVE PRONOUNS USED ALONE:
MINE, YOURS, HIS, HERS, ITS, OURS, THEIRS

Some possessive pronouns can stand alone: *mine, yours, his, hers, its, ours, theirs.*

Read each statement. Then fill in the blank with a possessive pronoun that can stand alone.

1. the girl's rabbit's foot   The rabbit's foot is _____.

2. my dog   The dog is _____.

3. Mom and Dad's scrapbook   The scrapbook is _____.

4. your book report   The book report is _____.

5. Jason's lucky stone   The stone is _____.

Circle the word in parentheses that correctly completes each sentence.

6. The story about the girl and her aunt is (hers, her's).

7. I wish that dancing dog were (my, mine)!

8. The ticket to the traveling show is (theirs, their's).

9. The last house on the right is (our's, ours).

10. Wei-Ling found a book of (yours, your's) near the swingset.

SENTENCE COMBINING WITH POSSESSIVE PRONOUNS

You may have to change possessive pronouns when you combine sentences.

Read each group of sentences. Then combine them into one sentence with a compound subject. Write the sentence on the lines. Change the possessive pronouns and any other words as needed.

1. Marcie turned in her book report. Heather turned in her book report, too.

_____

_____

2. The red dog is ours. So is the black and white one.

_____

_____

3. You can hang your jacket here. So can you.

_____

_____

4. The cassette tape on the desk is mine. The one on the chair is also mine.

_____

_____

5. I talked to my grandmother on Mother's Day. My sister did, too.

_____

_____

Macmillan/McGraw-Hill

ADJECTIVES

Each person has a family and group history. Very often we learn about our personal history from older members of our family. What have you learned about your history by talking with other people? Write a paragraph describing something you have learned about your personal or group history. Use adjectives in your paragraph.

_____

_____

_____

_____

_____

_____

_____

_____

_____

_____

_____

_____

_____

_____

_____

_____

_____

_____

_____

Macmillan/McGraw-Hill

Extension: Have students reread their paragraphs and underline each adjective they used.

ADJECTIVES THAT TELL *WHAT KIND*

> An **adjective** is a word that describes a noun. One type of adjective tells *what kind*.

Read through the adjectives that tell *what kind* in the list below. Then write a sentence using the subject in parentheses and an adjective from the list. Use each adjective only once. Cross out the adjective in the list as you use it in a sentence.

old	young	beautiful	loud	red
green	exciting	bright	heavy	brave
quiet	friendly	warm	clever	proud

1. (The mountains) _____

_____

2. (His sister) _____

_____

3. (The coyote) _____

_____

4. (The sun) _____

_____

5. (Grandfather) _____

_____

6. (A soldier) _____

_____

7. (Forests) _____

_____

8. (New York City) _____

9. (That jet) _____

10. (Our class) _____

Extension: Have students listen to the words of a favorite song and write down five adjectives that they hear in the lyrics.

10

Macmillan/McGraw-Hill

ADJECTIVES THAT TELL *HOW MANY*

An adjective is a word that describes a noun. One type of adjective tells *how many*.

Read each sentence. In the blank write an adjective from the list below that makes sense in the sentence. You may use some of the adjectives more than once.

many	three	no	several	fifty
few	seven hundred	two	most	all
one	each	some		

1. _____ students in our class are interested in history.

2. _____ girl wrote a report on her family history.

3. _____ students chose to write about our state's history.

4. Our state is one of _____ states in the United States.

5. _____ boys did a project on how Native Americans lived in our state.

6. My report was one of _____ reports on pioneer life.

7. _____ student is more interested in history than I am.

8. There were also _____ projects on our town.

9. _____ people lived in this town in the year 1900.

10. _____ person has his or her own history, too.

Extension: Have students read a section of their social studies book and copy each adjective that tells *how many*.

A, AN, THE

> The words *a, an,* and *the* are special adjectives called **articles**. Use *a* and *an* with singular nouns. Use *the* with singular nouns that name a particular person, place, or thing, and with all plural nouns.
>
> *The* Cedar River is one of *the* largest rivers in Iowa.
>
> *A* forest has *a* large number of trees.

There are clubs for just about any activity you can imagine. Write a paragraph about a club or organization you've joined. Did it turn out the way you planned? Use the articles *a, an,* and *the* at least ten times in your paragraph.

_____

_____

_____

_____

_____

_____

_____

_____

_____

_____

_____

_____

Extension: Have students exchange paragraphs and underline all the articles in the paragraph.

10

Macmillan/McGraw-Hill

ADJECTIVES AFTER LINKING VERBS

An adjective that follows a linking verb is called a **predicate adjective**.

Read each sentence. Underline each linking verb. Circle each predicate adjective.

1. Martina became very interested in history.

2. Martina is Mexican American.

3. Her ancestors were Mexican and Puerto Rican.

4. Martina is eager to learn about her people.

5. She feels proud of her people's history.

Complete each sentence by writing a predicate adjective. Then draw a line from the predicate adjective to the subject of the sentence that it is linked to.

6. My family's history seems _____.

7. I am American and _____.

8. My best friend's background is _____.

9. I feel _____ to know about my family's history.

10. Is your family's history _____?

Extension: Have students write three sentences about an older relative of theirs, using a predicate adjective in each one.

Name: _____   Date: _____

COMPARATIVE ADJECTIVES

The Fourth of July is a favorite holiday for many people in the United States. Write a paragraph comparing some of your favorite holidays. Tell which ones you like best, what you like about them, and how you celebrate them. Use comparative and superlative adjectives in your paragraph.

_____

_____

_____

_____

_____

_____

_____

_____

_____

_____

_____

_____

_____

_____

_____

_____

_____

_____

_____

_____

_____

_____

Extension: Have students exchange paragraphs and underline each comparative and superlative adjective. Then have them work together to make a list of synonyms for each adjective.

Macmillan/McGraw-Hill

COMPARATIVE ADJECTIVES: -ER OR MORE

Add -er to most adjectives to compare two nouns.
    Winter seems *longer* than summer.
With longer adjectives, use *more* to compare two nouns.
    I think basketball is *more exciting* than football.

Read each sentence. Underline each comparative adjective.

1. The sky is darker in the country than in the city.

2. Working in a steel mill is more dangerous than working in an office.

3. Pittsburgh, Pennsylvania, is larger than Weirton, West Virginia.

4. Nina is taller than Jason.

5. I am more interested in sports than Michael is.

Read each pair of words. Then write a sentence comparing the two items.
Use a comparative adjective in each sentence.

6. apple, orange _____

_____

7. moon, sun _____

_____

8. Dad, Grandfather _____

_____

9. dogs, cats _____

_____

10. science, math _____

_____

---

10   Level 10/Unit 5

Extension: Have students reread their answers for 6-10 and underline each comparative adjective.

97

SUPERLATIVE ADJECTIVES: -*EST* OR *MOST*

Add -*est* to most adjectives to compare more than two nouns.
   She is the *smallest* of the three kittens.
With longer adjectives, use *most* to compare more than two nouns.
   He is the *most unpredictable* teacher in the school.

Complete each sentence by writing the superlative form of the adjective in parentheses.

1. Cabbage rolls are the _____ food I know. (delicious)

2. The ride to Pittsburgh was the _____ trip I've ever taken! (sweaty)

3. Dad thinks the Pittsburgh Pirates are the _____ baseball team of all time. (great)

4. The steel mill makes the _____ noise I've ever heard. (loud)

5. The field trip to the steel mill was the _____ one our class has taken this year. (fascinating)

If the sentence uses the superlative form of an adjective correctly, write *C* on the line. If the sentence is incorrect, rewrite the word or words correctly on the line.

6. Zahara has the most shortest walk home from school. _____

7. The report about coal mining was the interestingest. _____

8. My dad always sings the funniest songs! _____

9. The hot dogs at Forbes Field in Pittsburgh are the most tastiest I've ever eaten! _____

10. After West Virginia, Illinois was the most flat place I'd ever seen.

_____

Extension Have students make a chart of five different adjectives, showing their positive, comparative, and superlative forms.

Level 10/Unit 5

10

Macmillan/McGraw-Hill

PROOFING PARAGRAPH WITH ADJECTIVES THAT COMPARE

> Add *-er* to most adjectives to compare two nouns. With longer adjectives, use *more* to compare two nouns.
> Add *-est* to most adjectives to compare more than two nouns. With longer adjectives, use *most* to compare more than two nouns.

Read the paragraph. Cross out each mistake with comparative and superlative adjectives. Then rewrite the paragraph on the lines, correcting each mistake.

      To me, the Fourth of July is the excitingest holiday of the year. I am probably more busier at that time than at any other time. I bet I've built most floats than anybody I know. Building a float in July can be hot work! That month is probably the most hot one in our state. Sometimes we work on the floats at night because it's coolest than in the day. It's a fantastic feeling when our float wins first prize in the parade.

_____

_____

_____

_____

_____

_____

_____

_____

_____

_____

_____

_____

Extension: Have students read a page of a favorite book and write out all the superlative and comparative adjectives.

COMPARATIVE ADJECTIVES

Add -*er* to most adjectives to compare two nouns. With longer adjectives, use *more* to compare two nouns.
Add -*est* to most adjectives to compare more than two nouns.
With longer adjectives, use *most* to compare more than two nouns.

Read each sentence. Circle the word in parentheses that correctly completes the sentence.

1. Brad's sister was the (littlest, most little) baton twirler in the parade.

2. Heather is two years (younger, youngest) than any of the other twirlers.

3. But she can throw her baton as (higher, high) as anyone in the group!

4. The Fourth of July parade is always the (more, most) exciting event of the summer in our town.

5. I think the clowns were (funnier, more funnier) last year.

6. The marching dogs from the kennel club were the (cuter, cutest) thing in the whole parade.

7. The mayor looked (happy, happier) than I'd ever seen him.

8. The TV weather reporter was the (most popular, popularest) person in the parade.

9. Which car was the (most slowest, slowest) in this year's parade?

10. That is the (most beautiful, beautifullest) horse I've ever seen!

Macmillan/McGraw-Hill

ADVERBS THAT TELL *HOW*

Almost everyone has had a pet at one time or another. Write a paragraph that describes a pet you have had or one you would like to have. Use adverbs in your paragraph.

_____

_____

_____

_____

_____

_____

_____

_____

_____

_____

_____

_____

_____

_____

_____

_____

_____

_____

WHAT IS AN ADVERB?

An **adverb** is a word that tells more about a verb.
   The cat crept *quietly* across the room.

Read each sentence. Circle each adverb. Then draw an arrow to the verb that the adverb tells more about.

1. The salesperson looked at the young girl curiously.

2. The fish happily ate the food.

3. Quickly, I hid the birthday gifts.

4. The rock star softly sang her song.

5. The woman in the cottage sews well.

6. Listen carefully while she reads the story.

7. Everyone ran quickly to the window.

8. Silently, he walked across the stage.

9. Did you copy the sentences correctly?

10. The unhappy girl sadly returned from the concert.

Extension: Have students work in pairs to write sentences for each other, then to add adverbs where appropriate.

Level 10/Unit 6

20

Macmillan/McGraw-Hill

ADVERBS THAT TELL *HOW*

Some adverbs tell how an action takes place. These adverbs usually end in *-ly*.
Julia spoke *softly* on the phone.

Read each sentence. Circle each adverb that tells *how*.

1. The stones sparkled beautifully in the moonlight.

2. The teacher looked at the baby lovingly.

3. We proudly walked into the stadium.

4. Quietly, she walked to the stairs and waited.

5. Everyone waited eagerly for the movie to start.

Complete each sentence by writing an adverb that tells *how*.

6. _____, the man continued his search for the puppy's owner.

7. You will be able to read this book if you plan your time
_____.

8. Work _____, but be careful.

9. _____, the girl chose the brown puppy.

10. She smiled _____ when she saw its floppy ears.

Extension: Have students read a section of their social studies book and copy each adverb that tells *how*.

Macmillan/McGraw-Hill

PLACEMENT OF ADVERBS THAT TELL *HOW* IN SENTENCES

Adverbs that tell *how* can be placed at the beginning of a sentence, before or after the verb they describe, or at the end of a sentence.
If you use an adverb at the beginning of a sentence, place a comma after it.

Add one adverb that tells *how* to each sentence and rewrite the sentence on the line.

1. If you look, you can see drawings of the city. _____

   _____

2. Pick up the injured bird. _____

   _____

3. We ran to the picnic shelter. _____

   _____

4. The crow screeched when it looked at us. _____

   _____

5. The dancers moved across the stage. _____

   _____

6. Mother reminded him to clean his room. _____

   _____

7. The story ends for all the mystery lovers. _____

   _____

8. She took the girl's jacket. _____

   _____

9. She cried when she found the coat was torn. _____

   _____

10. The artist draws horses. _____

    _____

USING *GOOD* AND *WELL* CORRECTLY

Good is an adjective. It tells about a noun.
   Tad is a *good* listener.
Well is an adverb. It describes a verb.
   He listens *well*.

Complete each sentence by writing *good* or *well*.

1. There are lots of _____ books about China.

2. Stories from other lands match the story of Cinderella quite _____.

3. In each tale, the young girl is kind and _____.

4. But her family does not treat her _____ at all.

5. The girl is a _____ dancer.

6. She dances so _____ at the ball that all eyes are

   on her.

7. There is usually someone who gives _____ advice.

8. The young girl follows the advice very _____.

9. But the stepmother makes a _____ plan.

10. The king or prince always has a _____ disguise.

Extension: Have students read an article in a newspaper or magazine and circle each use of *good* or *well*.

ADVERBS THAT TELL *WHERE* AND *WHEN*

Animals in stories are sometimes very different from real-life animals.

Use what you know about a pet or other animal to write a paragraph describing how the animal spends its time. What does it do all day?

Use adverbs in your paragraph that tell *where* and *when*.

_____

106 **Extension:** Have students exchange paragraphs and circle each *where* and *when* adverb.

Level 10/Unit 6

ADVERBS THAT TELL *WHERE*

Some adverbs tell where an action takes place. Some of these adverbs are *there, outside, up, here, nearby, ahead, around, far, away,* and *everywhere.*

Read through the adverbs that tell *where* in the list below. Then write a sentence using the subject in parentheses and an adverb from the list. Use each adverb only once. Cross out each adverb in the list as you use it in a sentence.

there	outside	up	here	nearby
ahead	around	somewhere	far	away
everywhere	inside	below	anywhere	above

1. (Beans) _____

_____

2. (Cornbread and honey) _____

_____

3. (The storyteller) _____

_____

4. (The pioneers) _____

_____

5. (You) _____

_____

6. (A snake) _____

_____

7. (Banjos, fiddles, and guitars) _____

_____

8. (Uncle Reuben) _____

9. (The hunting dogs) _____

10. (Tall trees) _____

Extension: Have students scan a favorite book and write down ten adverbs that tell *where.*

Macmillan/McGraw-Hill

ADVERBS THAT TELL *WHEN*

Some adverbs tell *when* an action takes place. Some of these adverbs are *now, first, always, next, after, tomorrow, soon, early, today, usually, then,* and *yesterday*.

Rewrite each sentence by adding an adverb that tells *when*.

1. The oldest son left home. _____

_____

2. He promised to write every week. _____

_____

3. "I'll be home for Thanksgiving," he told his family. _____

_____

4. Which son left home? _____

_____

5. Both sons joined the Navy. _____

_____

6. One learned about computers. _____

_____

7. "Will you be at this terminal?" he asked. _____

_____

8. "I believe I met your brother here," the instructor said. _____

_____

9. "I am not hungry," said the boy. _____

_____

10. "I'll eat at six o'clock!" said the student. _____

_____

Extension: Have students write their own sentences using five of the adverbs they added to the sentences above.

Level 10/Unit 6 10

PLACEMENT OF ADVERBS THAT TELL *WHERE* OR *WHEN* IN SENTENCES

> Adverbs that tell *where* or *when* can be put at the beginning of a sentence, before or after the verb they describe, or at the end of a sentence.
> If you use an adverb at the beginning of a sentence, place a comma after it.

Rewrite each sentence by adding an adverb that tells *where* or *when*. Add capital and lower-case letters as needed.

1. Melt some butter in the pan. _____

   _____

2. Take the meat out of the refrigerator. _____

   _____

3. Did you buy the meat at the grocery store? _____

   _____

4. Yes, I bought it. _____

   _____

5. We will have pork chops for dinner. _____

   _____

Write a sentence using the adverb in parentheses.

6. (outside) _____

7. (soon) _____

8. (always) _____

9. (nearby) _____

10. (up) _____

10   Level 10/Unit 6

Extension: Have students write lines from favorite songs that contain adverbs that tell *where* or *when*.

109

Macmillan/McGraw-Hill

ADVERBS THAT TELL *WHERE* AND *WHEN*

Some adverbs tell *where* an action takes place, such as *ahead* or *away*. Some adverbs tell *when* an action takes place, such as *early* and *soon*.
Adverbs that tell *where* or *when* can be put at the beginning of a sentence, before or after the verb, or at the end of a sentence.

Write a sentence using the adverb in parentheses. At the end of the sentence, write *where* or *when* to describe what the adverb tells.

1. (here) _____
   _____

2. (usually) _____
   _____

3. (up) _____
   _____

4. (everywhere) _____
   _____

5. (then) _____
   _____

6. (before) _____
   _____

7. (far) _____
   _____

8. (early) _____
   _____

9. (today) _____

10. (there) _____

Extension: Have students work together to make a two-column list of *where* and *when* adverbs. Then have them take turns using the words in sentences.

Macmillan/McGraw-Hill

ADVERBS THAT COMPARE

Think about your parents and grandparents, brothers and sisters, aunts and uncles, and even your cousins. Does one person sing better, work harder, or run faster than the others? Write a paragraph that compares how some members of your family do things differently. Use adverbs that compare in your paragraph.

_____

_____

_____

_____

_____

_____

_____

_____

_____

_____

_____

_____

_____

_____

_____

_____

_____

_____

Extension: Have students exchange paragraphs and underline each adverb that compares.

ADVERBS THAT COMPARE *HOW*

Add *-er* or use *more* when you compare two actions. Add *-est* or use *most* when you compare more than two actions.

Read each sentence. If the sentence uses adverbs that compare *how* correctly, write *C* on the line. If the sentence is incorrect, rewrite it correctly on the line.

1. Which of Jenna's two sisters sings more sweetly? _____

_____

2. One sister acts most kindly than the other. _____

_____

3. She practices more careful than her sister. _____

_____

4. Tomas reads the fastest of anyone in our class. _____

_____

5. These crops grew quicklier than those over there. _____

_____

6. Conchita sews more better than Ramona. _____

_____

7. I would be a good sewer if I worked more slow. _____

_____

8. We finished our section of the quilt easier than any other group. _____

_____

112 **Extension:** Have students reread their answers and write *2* above those adverbs that compare two actions and *3* over those that compare more than two actions.

Level 10/Unit 6

8

Macmillan/McGraw-Hill

ADVERBS THAT COMPARE *WHERE*

Add *-er* or use *more* when you compare two actions. Add *-est* or use *most* when you compare more than two actions.

Read the adverbs that compare *where* in the list below. Then complete each sentence by writing in the blank the correct form of an adverb that compares *where*. You may use the adverbs more than once.

far   near   close   high   low

1. My mom's parents live _____ to us than my dad's

    parents.

2. Which airplane flew the _____?

3. Move your sleeping bag _____ to the campfire.

4. I threw the ball the _____ of anyone in the contest.

5. Which cat sleeps _____ to the bed, Winky or Mittens?

6. Who can sing the _____ in the choir?

7. The red squirrel climbed _____ in the maple tree

    than the gray one.

8. Which of your friends lives the _____ to you?

9. This pitcher throws the ball _____ than the last

    pitcher.

10. Lateeka lives _____ to me of all my good friends.

Extension: Have students read a section of a newspaper or magazine and copy all
the comparative adverbs they find.

ADVERBS THAT COMPARE *WHEN*

Add *-er* or use *more* when you compare two actions. Add *-est* or use *most* when you compare more than two actions.

Read the adverbs that compare *when* in the list below. Then complete each sentence by writing in the blank the correct form of an adverb that compares *when*. You may use the adverbs more than once.

soon   late   early   frequently   recently   often

1. The first sister arrived in the city _____ than the other.

2. You can come to the meeting _____ if you don't want to hear the speech.

3. I walk to school _____ than I ride my bike.

4. The postcard got here from Africa _____ than I expected.

5. Which movie have you seen _____: *Jaws, Raiders of the Lost Ark*, or *Batman*?

6. We see our cousins _____ than most people since they live across the street.

7. What is the _____ you can come to the game?

8. Chris handed in her test _____ of all.

9. Dad watches basketball the _____ of all sports.

10. Whoever arrives the _____ will win the door prize.

Extension: Have students quiz each other by naming an adverb that tells *when* and having the other make up a sentence using both comparative and superlative forms.

Level 10/Unit 6

10

Macmillan/McGraw-Hill

ADVERBS THAT COMPARE

An adverb can compare two or more actions.
Add -er or use *more* when you compare two actions.
Add -est or use *most* when you compare more than two actions.

Write a sentence using the adverb in parentheses.

1. (quickest) _____

_____

2. (more often) _____

_____

3. (loudest) _____

_____

4. (closer) _____

_____

5. (highest) _____

_____

6. (more carefully) _____

_____

7. (most recently) _____

_____

8. (farther) _____

_____

9. (earliest) _____

_____

10. (fastest) _____

Macmillan/McGraw-Hill

DOUBLE NEGATIVES

Have you ever thought about what it means to be satisfied with your life? Write five rules you think a person should follow to be satisfied. Two examples are "Don't be jealous of your friends" and "Don't always wish you could be someone else." Use a negative in each of your rules.

1. _____

   _____

2. _____

   _____

3. _____

   _____

4. _____

   _____

5. _____

   _____

Extension: Have students exchange lists of rules and circle each negative. Then have them rewrite the rules without the negatives, expressing them in a positive way.

116

Level 10/Unit 6

5

COMMON NEGATIVES: *NO, NONE, NOWHERE, NOT, NEVER, NOBODY, NOTHING*

> A **negative** is a word that means *no*. Never use two negatives in the same sentence.

Read the paragraph. Circle each incorrect negative. Then rewrite the paragraph, using negatives correctly.

Cutting stone is not no easy job. Nothing is not harder than stone to cut, shape, and polish. Nobody can't imagine how difficult it can be. In addition, nowhere is not a harder place to work than on a mountainside. There is no job that does not take more skill than cutting stone.

_____
_____
_____
_____
_____
_____
_____
_____
_____
_____
_____
_____
_____

Extension: Have students scan a page from a book of their choice. Ask them to copy the negative words they find on a sheet of paper.

117

COMMON NEGATIVE CONTRACTIONS: *CAN'T, DON'T, WON'T*

A **negative** is a word that means *no.* Never use two negatives in the same sentence.

Read each sentence. Fill in the blank with *can't, don't,* or *won't.*

1. Camels _____ need to drink water for long periods of time.

2. The caravan _____ pass because of the terrible sandstorm.

3. It _____ be able to leave until tomorrow.

4. We _____ see with all this sand blowing in the air.

5. I hope tomorrow _____ be like this in the desert.

Write a sentence using the negative contraction in parentheses.

6. (won't) _____

_____

7. (can't) _____

_____

8. (don't) _____

_____

9. (won't) _____

_____

10. (can't) _____

_____

Extension: Have students listen to the lyrics of a favorite song and write down all the negatives they hear.

Level 10/Unit 6

10

Macmillan/McGraw-Hill

COMMON NEGATIVE CONTRACTIONS:
COULDN'T, DOESN'T, SHOULDN'T

> A **negative** is a word that means *no*. Never use two negatives in the same sentence.

Read each sentence. Then rewrite it using *couldn't, doesn't,* or *shouldn't* so that it means the opposite.

1. People should be unhappy with their work. _____

   _____

2. They could do well if they were worried. _____

   _____

3. The merchant should stop for rest and refreshment. _____

   _____

4. The engineer likes his work on the mountainside. _____

   _____

5. He could be famous. _____

6. The sun beats down on a foggy day. _____

   _____

7. You should gaze at the sun. _____

8. Even sunglasses could protect your eyes. _____

   _____

9. The wind breaks up the clouds. _____

   _____

10. The wind could be blocked by a mountain. _____

    _____

Extension: Have students work in pairs to list negative and positive words that can be used instead of nouns. Examples: *nobody, somebody, nothing,* and *something.*

119

DOUBLE NEGATIVES

A **negative** is a word that means *no*. Never use two negatives in the same sentence.

Read each sentence. Then rewrite it, correcting the double negatives.

1. Nothing can't move a mountain. _____

   _____

2. Doesn't no one want to be a stonecutter? _____

   _____

3. The night is so cloudy I can't see nothing. _____

   _____

4. You won't never be able to ride that camel! _____

   _____

5. Nobody wouldn't help me polish this block of stone. _____

   _____

6. We haven't never eaten anything so delicious as a sherbet. _____

   _____

7. I would offer you a sherbet, but there aren't none left. _____

   _____

8. No one couldn't keep the sun from burning the king's skin. _____

   _____

9. There isn't no reason why he should be so unhappy. _____

   _____

10. The stonecutter wouldn't wear no shoes but slippers. _____

    _____

Extension: Have students write three sentences that contain double negatives like those above and have a partner correct them.

Macmillan/McGraw-Hill